Nicaragua Style

Recipes

A Complete Cookbook of Latin American Dish Ideas!

BY

Julia Chiles

OOOOOOOOOOOOOOOOOOOOOOOOOOOOOOOOOOOOOOO

License Notes

No part of this Book can be reproduced in any form or by any means including print, electronic, scanning or photocopying unless prior permission is granted by the author.

All ideas, suggestions and guidelines mentioned here are written for informative purposes. While the author has taken every possible step to ensure accuracy, all readers are advised to follow information at their own risk. The author cannot be held responsible for personal and/or commercial damages in case of misinterpreting and misunderstanding any part of this Book

OOOOOOOOOOOOOOOOOOOOOOOOOOOOOOOOOOOOOOO

Table of Contents

Introduction

The cuisine of Nicaragua includes numerous foods dating back to many different cultures that trace to pre-Columbian cooking. Other recipes were brought to Nicaragua by settlers from Europe over the last few hundred years.

Especially influential in Nicaraguan cuisine are recipes and cooking methods from Germany and Spain. Spanish settlers brought along their cooking methods when they were colonizing this area of Central America.

Germans have also been quite successful in Nicaragua. Their methods of food preparation and cooking had an influence on the country. Some staples in Nicaraguan cuisine were introduced to the country from Germans, including wheat, plantains and yams.

The average Nicaraguan has a diet centered heavily around chicken, Gallo pinto and corn tortillas. Gallo pinto is a blend of rice and beans that is the basis of many dishes made by locals in Nicaragua. It is fairly inexpensive, and easy for most people to afford.

Fish, pork and beef are also used in Nicaraguan dishes. Plantains are used a great deal, in many delicious ways. Oddly, Nicaraguans enjoy eating some fruits before they ripen, likely to make use of it before it dies. The reasoning isn't as clear as the fact that it makes their dishes more interesting. Try some of these intriguing dishes soon!

Breakfasts

Breakfast is a time to take in sustenance for the busy day ahead in Nicaragua. Here are a few favorite breakfast recipes…

1 – Rice Bean Breakfast – Gallo Pinto

This is a fairly basic recipe for Gallo Pinto. It is cooked on most mornings, and sometimes is topped with a slice of bacon and a fried egg.

Makes 4 Servings

Cooking + Prep Time: 1/2 hour

Ingredients:

- 3 tbsp. of oil, vegetable
- 1 tbsp. of lizano salsa
- 1 1/2 cups of cooked beans, black
- 2 1/2 cups of cooked rice
- 2 tbsp. of chopped bell peppers
- 2 tbsp. of chopped onions
- 1 tbsp. of chopped coriander

Instructions:

1. Sauté the pepper and onion for two minutes or so.

2. Add salsa and black beans. Simmer over med. heat for 10-12 minutes.

3. Add cooked rice and coriander and mix well.

4. Add items you enjoy, like sausage, chicken, pork, bacon and/or eggs. Serve.

2 – Fresh Breakfast Corn Cakes - Tamales de elote

This is another favorite breakfast dish in Nicaragua. It's also popular in Mexico and elsewhere in Central America. Their corn is higher in starch than Western countries but adding masa harina makes it more similar to typical corn.

Makes 12 Servings

Cooking + Prep Time: 2 hours 40 minutes

Ingredients:

- 12-15 corn husks, to wrap
- 1/4 cup of lard
- 1/4 cup of softened butter, unsalted
- 2 tsp. of baking powder
- 2 cups of masa harina (traditional Latin American flour)
- 1 cup of water, warm
- 2 tsp. of salt, kosher
- 2-3 ears of corn on cob

Instructions:

1. Add corn husks to large sized pot. Cover with boiling water. Allow them to soak for 1/2 hour or longer.

2. Add butter, baking powder and lard to food processor. Melt till fluffy and light.

3. Cut 2 cups of corn kernels from cobs. Add to food processor. Pulse till somewhat smooth, but with a few chunks remaining.

4. Mix warm water, masa harina and salt together in large sized bowl. Knead till you have a mass that is pliable. Pulse into lard and corn mixture in small amounts till the mixture has a smooth texture.

5. Drain corn husks. Wipe them dry. Lay out one husk with its pointed end facing upwards. Add 1/4 cup of dough to middle. Fold in sides and cover dough. Fold up bottom. Fold down pointed top. Insert into bottom fold to create a packet. Tie if desired. Repeat this step with the remainder of dough.

6. Set up steamer. Steam tamales for 35-45 minutes, then remove them. Pour a bit of cream or milk on top of tamales and serve hot.

3 – Corn Pancakes - Güirilas

These are a little bit salty and a little bit sweet. When you combine them with curd cheese (cuajada), it is one of the most delightful of Nicaraguan dishes.

Makes 8 Servings

Cooking + Prep Time: 25 minutes

Ingredients:

- 1 1/2 cups of sweet corn mix (P.A.N.)
- 2 1/2 cups of milk, low fat
- 2 tbsp. of sugar, granulated
- 8 x 8-inch plantain leaves
- 1 tsp. of salt, kosher

Instructions:

1. Mix the milk, salt and sugar in medium bowl. Add sweet corn mix slowly and stir constantly while adding it. Cover the batter with clean dish cloth. Allow to rest for five minutes.

2. Place eight plantain leaves on work surface. Pour 1 tbsp. of batter in middles. Cover using other eight leaves. Cook in pan till both sides are golden brown in color. Serve hot.

Lunch, Dinner, Side Dish and Appetizer Recipes

Nicaraguans have some wonderful lunch, dinner, side dish and appetizer recipes. Here are some of the best...

4 – Nicaraguan Almond Soup – Ajo Blanco

This old almond soup is rather like a gazpacho alternative. This version relies totally on the texture and flavor of almonds and garlic.

Makes 4 Servings

Cooking + Prep Time: 45 minutes

Ingredients:

- 6 cups of almonds, whole
- 4 cups of ice cubes in water
- 1 clove of garlic
- 2 tbsp. of oil, olive
- 1 tbsp. of vinegar, sherry wine
- 1 pinch salt, sea
- 3 cups of de-seeded, cubed watermelon
- 1 tbsp. of oil, basil-infused

Instructions:

1. Place the almonds in food processor. Blitz till you have created fine-textured almond meal.

2. Transfer the mixture to blender. Add ice cubes and cold water.

3. Blend for one to two minutes till ice is crushed completely.

4. Add olive oil, sea salt, vinegar and garlic. Continue to blend for a couple more minutes.

5. Taste soup. You want it creamy.

6. Adjust the ingredients if needed.

7. Place watermelon cubes in four individual bowls.

8. Pour cold soup over cubes till almost covered fully.

9. Garnish using basil-infused oil and olive oil.

10. Serve promptly.

5 - Ceviche

This recipe is widely used, in Nicaragua, Costa Rica and other South American and Latin American countries. The seafood in the dish is cooked by means of lime juice. The freshest ingredients will make a wonderful dish.

Makes 4 Servings

Cooking + Prep Time: 1/2 hour + 8 hours chilling time

Ingredients:

- 1 lb. of scallops, bay
- 8 fresh limes, juice only
- 2 sliced stalks of celery
- 5 minced scallions
- 2 tomatoes, diced
- 1/2 minced bell pepper, green
- 1/2 cup chopped parsley, fresh
- Pepper, black, ground
- 1 1/2 tbsp. oil, olive
- 1/8 cup chopped cilantro, fresh

Instructions:

1. Rinse the scallops. Place in medium bowl. Pour the lime juice over them till they are immersed completely.

2. Chill scallops in lime juice for 8-12 hours till scallops have become opaque.

3. Empty 1/2 lime juice from scallop bowl. Add the cilantro, olive oil, ground pepper, parsley, bell pepper, celery, green onions and tomatoes. Gently stir.

4. Pour into fancy glasses and serve.

6 – Nicaraguan Fish Soup - Sopa de Pescado

Fish soup is a cheap, light, delicious, healthy alternative to soups that are built around meat. If your young children don't like fish, this recipe is just the thing to change their minds.

Makes 6 Servings

Cooking + Prep Time: 1/2 hour

Ingredients:

- 1 1/2 pounds of sea bass or any other local fish
- 2 tbsp. oil, olive
- 1 fresh lime, juice only
- 2 sliced garlic cloves
- 1 diced carrot, large
- 1 cup diced potatoes
- 1 cup diced auyama (also known as a West Indian pumpkin)
- 2 quarts of water, filtered
- 2 cilantro sprigs
- 1 1/2 tsp. of salt, + more, if desired

Instructions:

1. Mix 1/2 of fish with pumpkin, potatoes, carrots, garlic, lime juice and oil. Add 1/2 water. Cook on med. heat till vegetables have cooked through fully.

2. Remove as many fish bones as you can. Add the rest of the water, fish and cilantro. Cook on lowest heat till just-added fish has cooked through fully. Season as desired. Serve hot.

7 – Cassava Fries - Yuca Frita

Yuca is such a staple vegetable in the Caribbean and Latin America. It's starchy, so it's often used like Western chefs use potatoes.

Makes 3-5 Servings

Cooking + Prep Time: 1 1/2 hour

Ingredients:

- 1 1/2 lbs. of cassava (yuca) root
- Water, filtered, to boil
- Oil, olive, to fry
- Salt, kosher, as desired

Instructions:

1. Bring large sized pot of lightly salted water to boil. Peel brown skin from yuca. Cut yuca in large sized chunks. Do not use stringy center.

2. Next, add yuca to boiling water. Cook for 18-20 minutes or so. Drain. Spread yuca out on clean towel. Allow to dry for 12-15 minutes.

3. Heat deep-frying oil till it shimmers. Fry yuca in small batches till golden brown in color. Remove to plate lined with paper towels. Place in warm oven on metal pan and keep warm until all batches are fried. Season as desired. Serve.

8 – Chicken Rice Stew - Arroz Aguado

This is a variation on original Nicaraguan chicken soup. It is laden with chicken pieces and seasonal vegetables. The cilantro **Makes** it unique.

Makes 6 Servings

Cooking + Prep Time: 1 hour 20 minutes

Ingredients:

- 2 tbsp. of oil, vegetable
- 1/2 chopped onion, medium
- 3 chopped cloves of garlic
- 2 tbsp. of chili paste, if desired
- 1/2 cup of cilantro, mixed with 2 tbsp. of filtered water
- 4 skinless chicken thighs
- 1 skinless chicken breast
- 1/2 cup each of cubed bell pepper, red and yellow
- 1 cup of peas
- 1 1/2 cups of corn, whole kernel
- 1 cup of cooked green beans
- 2 cups of beer, your favorite type/brand
- 4 cups of stock, chicken
- Salt, kosher
- Pepper, black, ground
- 2 cups of rice, Arborio
- Onion and bell pepper sauce

Instructions:

1. Heat oil in medium pot on high heat.

2. Add garlic and onion. Fry for several minutes, till they appear soft. Add blended cilantro and chili paste. Allow to cook for several minutes.

3. Add chicken. Stir thoroughly. Add chicken breast and thighs. Add bell pepper, corn, peas, green beans, chicken stock and beer. Season as desired.

4. Cover pot. Allow the stew to cook for 20-25 minutes. Remove part of stock and chicken breast. Set them aside.

5. Continue to cook for 20 minutes more. Add rice. Stir thoroughly. Cook on low heat till rice has cooked al dente. Serve with onion and bell pepper sauce.

9 – Shredded Beef Salad - Salpicon de Res

This refreshing Central American salad works wonderfully wrapped in corn tortillas or as a hearty topping for corn tortillas. It's easy to make large batches, so it's super for family gatherings and parties.

Makes 4-6 Servings

Cooking + Prep Time: 2 3/4 hours

Ingredients:

- 2 – 2 1/2 lbs. of skirt steak or beef flank steak
- 1 chopped onion
- 1/3 cup of oil, olive
- 1/4 cup of vinegar
- 1-2 tsp. of oregano
- Salt, kosher, as desired
- Pepper, black, ground, as desired
- 3 de-seeded, chopped tomatoes
- 1 thinly sliced onion
- 3 minced chilies, Serrano
- 2 chopped avocados

Instructions:

1. Add onion, salt and beef to large sized pot. Cover with water. Bring to boil, then reduce the heat to med-low. Simmer for 1 1/4 – 2 hours. Meat should be quite tender.

2. Remove meat. Reserve stock for another recipe. Allow meat to cool and then use fingers to shred it.

3. Add vinegar, olive oil, kosher salt, ground pepper and oregano to large sized bowl. Whisk together well. Add chilies, tomatoes and sliced onion. Toss together and set aside for several minutes so veggies can marinate.

4. Toss avocados and shredded beef gently with veggies. Season as desired. Spread out on serving platter. Serve at room temperature or chill and serve.

10 – Nicaraguan-Style Cheese Soup - Sopa de Queso Nicaragüense

This is a traditional Lenten soup from the Roman Catholics of Nicaragua, when meat cannot be eaten. If not observing Lent, you can use chicken stock instead of vegetable stock.

Makes 2-3 Servings

Cooking + Prep Time: 35 minutes

Ingredients:

- 7 cups stock, vegetable
- 1/2 cup cream, Latin style
- 2 cups milk, whole

Instructions:

1. Bring vegetable stock to simmer in large Dutch oven.

2. Add milk. Bring back up to simmer.

3. Remove 1/2 stock. Place in large sized bowl.

4. Add cream and 1 cup masa.

5. Mix well. Add to stock for thickening.

6. Season as desired. Serve.

11 – Beef Turnovers - Empanadas

Served often in Nicaragua and Costa Rica, this is a perfect meal in a pastry. They are beef turnovers, and this recipe also includes garlic, onions and egg.

Makes 4-6 Servings

Cooking + Prep Time: 40 minutes

Ingredients:

- 1 tbsp. of oil, olive
- 1/2 lb. of beef steak, ground
- 1/4-lb. of chorizo sausage, fresh, with removed casing
- 3/4 cup of onion, chopped
- 2 chopped garlic cloves
- 1/4 tsp. of cumin, ground
- 1/2 tsp. of salt, kosher
- 1/2 tsp. of pepper, black, ground
- 1 pkg. of pie crust, store bought
- 1 egg, large

Instructions:

1. Preheat oven to 375F.

2. Heat oil on high heat in med. skillet. Add chorizo, beef, garlic, onion, cumin, kosher salt ground pepper.

3. Cook for five to seven minutes and stir constantly, to blend ingredients well. Set aside. Allow the filling to cool.

4. Roll pie crust dough out. Cut rounds with 3" cutter. Place 1 tbsp. filling on 1/2 rounds. Fold other halves around and over. Press on dough edges with fork, to be sure you have sealed them.

5. Whisk egg in bowl and brush empanada tops with egg wash. Arrange empanadas on baking pan. Bake till they have a golden-brown color. Transfer to platter. Serve hot.

12 – Seafood Coconut Soup

This delicious soup combines fresh vegetables and seafood to provide a taste that's a little bit sweet. It's another recipe that the whole family loves.

Makes 4 Servings

Cooking + Prep Time: 35 minutes

Ingredients:

- 32 ounces of stock, chicken
- 10 sliced button mushrooms
- 1/2 cup of chopped kale
- 1 cup of chopped lettuce, romaine
- 4 chunk-cut filets, tilapia
- 10 prawns or shrimp
- Optional: 10 mussels
- Optional: 1 tsp. of fish sauce
- 1 cup of cream, coconut, from canned coconut milk
- Salt, sea, as desired

Instructions:

1. Pour stock in large sized pot. Bring to a boil.

2. Add lettuce, mushrooms and kale. Bring back to boil.

3. Add tilapia chunks, prawns/shrimp and bring back to boil. Be sure your soup has covered all seafood. Add additional stock if you need it.

4. Boil for about four minutes till prawns/shrimp are pink and chunks of tilapia are not translucent anymore.

5. Add fish sauce and sea salt, if desired. Add coconut cream. Stir and mix, without breaking up the pieces of fish a lot.

6. As soon as soup barely starts boiling again, remove from heat. Serve promptly.

13 – Latin-American Fried Plantains - Plátanos Fritos

This recipe is popular in countries of Latin America, where it is used as a source of calories from starch. The dish requires ripe plantains, with black skins, since green plantains would be too dry.

Makes 3-5 Servings

Cooking + Prep Time: 25 minutes

Ingredients:

- 4 plantains, ripe, peeled, halved cross-ways, then lengthways
- To fry – oil, olive

Instructions:

1. Heat 1/2" oil in skillet on med. heat. Add plantains. Sauté till browned lightly. Sauté other side.

2. Remove plantains to plate lined with paper towels. Repeat with remainder of plantains and sprinkle with a bit of salt. Then serve hot.

14 – Nicaraguan Steak Skewers

People in Central America never seem to tire of grilled meat. This dish pairs skewers of grilled, spiced tenderloin with tasty chimichurri sauce.

Makes 8 Servings

Cooking + Prep Time: 1 hour 5 minutes + 4 hours total marinating time

Ingredients:

- 3/4 pound of beef steak, trimmed to 1" thickness

For chimichurri

- 2 cups of parsley, fresh
- 4 cloves of garlic
- 1/4 cup of oil, olive
- 2 tbsp. of vinegar, white wine
- 3/4 tsp. of salt, kosher
- 1/2 tsp. of pepper, ground

Instructions:

1. To prepare chimichurri, place vinegar, oil, kosher salt, ground pepper, garlic and parsley in food processor. Process till it forms a smooth-textured paste.

2. Reserve 1/4 cup of chimichurri. Place remainder in sealed container in fridge to let the flavors blend for two hours or longer.

3. To prepare beef, place steak in zipper top plastic bag. Add reserved 1/4 cup chimichurri. Seal bag. Massage marinade into meat. Allow meat to marinate for two hours or longer.

4. Preheat grill to medium. Place marinated meat on grill. Cover. Cook for three to four minutes on first side. Flip meat. Cook for three to four more minutes on second side.

5. When it's done, the meat will still be a bit soft. Remove from grill. Allow it to rest on work surface for 10-12 minutes, so juices can settle.

6. Thinly slice steak angled across grain. Thread the thin slices of meat on toothpicks and serve along with chimichurri sauce.

15 – Carne Asada – Grilled Meat

"Carne asada" is the Spanish term for "grilled meat", so this recipe is not too complicated. It offers great back yard BBQ food that's tender and smoky.

Makes 4-6 Servings

Cooking + Prep Time: 55 minutes + 8 hours marinating time

Ingredients:

- 2-3 lbs. of skirt or flank steak
- 1-2 sliced onions
- 2-3 oranges, only juice
- Salt, kosher and pepper, ground, as desired
- 1/4 cup of oil

Instructions:

1. Mix meat with orange juice, onions, oil, kosher salt and ground pepper in large glass bowl. Cover. Marinate it overnight.

2. Start a fire in grill. Remove meat from marinade and pat it dry. Grill over the hot flame till first side has browned well.

3. Turn meat over. Grill on second side. Remove to work surface. Allow to rest for 10 minutes or more.

4. Slice meat thinly across grain, making strips. Serve.

16 – Pork Rinds Cassava Root – Nicaraguan Vigoron

Nicaraguan Vigoron consists of boiled cassava root (yuca) topped with cabbage salad and pork rinds. You can serve it as a light dinner or appetizer.

Makes 4-6 Servings

Cooking + Prep Time: 50 minutes

Ingredients:

- 2 lbs. of cassava (yuca root), fresh
- 1 x 16 to 18-ounce bag of cabbage salad (coleslaw mix)
- 1 lb. of pork rinds

Instructions:

1. Cut ends of yuca root with sharp knife. Cut into 4" chunks. Slice skin off. Rinse and place in large sized pot.

2. Fill the pot with water, covering yuca fully. Set on med-high. Bring to simmer. Cook till fork tender, which usually takes about 1/2 hour. Don't overcook yuca or it will turn mushy.

3. After yuca has cooked, remove from water. Place on work surface. Cut in bite-sized cubes. Discard fibrous parts.

4. To assemble, place pieces of yuca on plates or in bowls. Top using cabbage salad and pork rinds. Serve promptly.

17 – Chorizo, Pork Tripe Soup - Sopa de Mondongo

A variety of vegetables and meats come together in mondongo. They're cooked together till everything in your stock pot is luscious and fork tender.

Makes 6-8 Servings

Cooking + Prep Time: 3 hours 15 minutes

Ingredients:

- 1 lb. of small-cubed mondongo (beef tripe)
- 1 fresh lime, juice only
- 1/4 tsp. of baking soda
- 1 1/2 lbs. of small-cubed pork
- Optional: 3 sliced chorizos
- 1 chopped tomato
- 2 chopped scallions
- 1/4 cup of chopped onion, white
- 4 diced potatoes, small
- 1 lb. of diced yuca
- Salt, kosher
- Pepper, black, ground
- 1/2 tsp. of cumin, ground
- 1/4 tsp. of achiote
- 1/3 cup of cilantro, fresh
- 1 chopped clove of garlic
- Water, filtered

Instructions:

1. Wash tripe using warm water. Rub it with fresh lime juice. Combine tripe with baking soda and water sufficient to cover tripe + two inches in large sized pot.

2. Bring water to boil. Then reduce to simmer. Cook till tripe has become very tender. This takes between 1 1/2 and 2 hours. Drain tripe. Discard water.

3. Place cooked tripe, chorizos, pork meat, onion, scallions, tomato, achiote, garlic and cumin in another large sized pot. Add water sufficient to cover them all.

4. Bring to boil. Reduce to low heat. Slowly simmer for 40-45 minutes. Then add potatoes, yuca and cilantro. Cook for 1/2 hour longer.

5. Ladle the soup into bowls. Garnish with lime wedges and extra cilantro. Serve.

18 – Run Down Soup - Rondon

This is a yummy stew that is prepared from what you have at home or catch that day. This traditionally meant the fish that the fishermen caught that day and some meat from local wild birds and wild boar. My ingredients are a little more mundane.

Makes 2 large servings

Cooking + Prep Time: 1 hour 55 minutes

Ingredients:

- 1 yuca root (cassava)
- 1 sweet potato
- 1 bread fruit
- 1 unripe banana
- 1 plantain
- 1 onion, yellow
- 1 yucca
- 1 garlic clove
- 1 China pepper
- 1 lobster tail
- 1 handful shrimp
- 1 fish, white or mild
- 1 handful of basil
- 1 handful of marjoram
- 1 scoop of consume, chicken
- 1 lime, fresh
- 2 coconuts, dry

Instructions:

1. Peel all the veggies except for the sweet potato. Cut them into halves.

2. Add the lime to water in large pot. This will keep the bananas from becoming brown. Soak the cut veggies for 1/2 hour.

3. Shred the coconut in a medium bowl. Add water. Squeeze the shredded coconut.

4. Drain the water and coconut through sieve into large sized pot for soup.

5. Peel the leaves from basil and marjoram and soak for about five minutes.

6. Add basil and marjoram to the coconut milk. Place on stove and boil.

7. Add the scoop of consume to the ingredients on stove.

8. Add onion and garlic to the mixture.

9. Once mixture boils, add all the root vegetables. Cook for 20-25 minutes.

10. Clean the seafood. Steam it on top of the soup for last 10 minutes. Don't break fish apart when you stir the mixture. Serve in big bowls with limes on side.

19 – Chicken with Pineapple Olives - Chicken Costa Brava

This chicken dish was influenced by Spain's northern region of Costa Brava and their cuisine. It marries the tropical, sweet flavor of pineapple with chicken and the saltiness of olives. It tastes great over rice.

Makes 10 Servings

Cooking + Prep Time: 1 hour 40 minutes

Ingredients:

- 1 x 20-oz. can of chunked pineapple
- 10 halved chicken breasts, boneless, skinless
- 1 tbsp. of oil, vegetable
- 1 tsp. of cumin, ground
- 1 tsp. of cinnamon, ground
- 2 minced garlic cloves
- 1 quartered onion
- 1 x 14 1/2-oz. can of tomatoes, stewed
- 2 cups of olives, black, pitted
- 1/2 cup of salsa
- 2 tbsp. of corn starch
- 2 tbsp. of water, filtered
- 1 sliced bell pepper, red
- Salt, kosher, as desired

Instructions:

1. Drain the pineapple and reserve the juice. Season as desired.

2. Brown chicken in the oil in large sized fry pan. Combine cinnamon and cumin. Sprinkle it over the chicken.

3. Add the onion and garlic. Cook till the onion has become soft. Add the pineapple juice, along with tomatoes, salsa and olives. Cover pan. Simmer for 25-30 minutes.

4. Mix the corn starch with filtered water. Stir it into the juices in pan. Add the bell pepper. Simmer till the sauce has boiled and thickened. Add and stir pineapple chunks. Heat through well and serve.

20 – Nicaraguan Steak Churrasco

This main dish is a grilled tenderloin with garlic and chimichurri sauce. It's very flavorful, the meat is tender and it comes together very quickly.

Makes 4-6 Servings

Cooking + Prep Time: 45 minutes

Ingredients:

- 1 1/2 pounds of center cut steaks, beef tenderloin
- 1 bunch of fresh Italian parsley, large
- 4 peeled cloves of garlic
- 1 cup of oil, olive
- 1/4 cup of vinegar, red wine, +/- as desired
- 3 tbsp. of water, filtered
- 1 1/2 tsp. of salt, kosher, as desired
- 1 tsp. of ground pepper, black, as desired

Instructions:

1. Place tenderloin lengthways on your work surface. Cut into four even, flat horizontal strips and place each of them between sheets of cling wrap. Pound with side of cleaver till thickness is 1/4 inch. Then arrange steaks in glass casserole dish.

2. Combine garlic and parsley in food processor. Process till chopped finely. Add 1/4 cup of vinegar, all the oil, and season as desired. Process, creating a thicker sauce. Season as desired again. Mixture needs a good amount of seasoning.

3. Place 1/2 of this chimichurri sauce in bowl to serve from. Pour remainder of sauce over meat. Cover meat. Allow to marinate in fridge for 1/2 hour. Turn a few times while marinating.

4. Preheat your grill for high heat. Oil the grate.

5. Drain beef. Place on grate as soon as it is hot. Grill and turn with the tongs, till cooked as you desire. Serve with the rest of your chimichurri sauce.

21 – Plantain Hash - Picadillo de Platano

This is a delectable plantain hash dish that a friend brought back from a visit to Central America. It can be served as a side or on a nice, hot tortilla.

Makes 8 Servings

Cooking + Prep Time: 1 1/4 hour

Ingredients:

- 4 peeled plantains, cut in three pieces
- 1/2 lb. of beef, ground
- 2 minced garlic cloves
- 2 tbsp. of onion, minced
- 2 tsp. of salt, kosher
- 1/2 tsp. of pepper, ground
- 1 1/2 tbsp. of cilantro, chopped
- 1/2 cup of chopped tomato
- 2 tsp. of Worcestershire sauce
- 1 dash of pepper sauce, hot

Instructions:

1. Simmer plantains in lightly salted, filtered water on med-high till they become tender. Then drain them, allow them to cool, and chop finely.

2. Heat the oil in large sized skillet on med-high. Add and stir beef, onion and garlic. Season as desired. Cook till onion becomes soft and beef crumbly. Add and stir tomato, plantain and cilantro. Season using hot pepper sauce and Worcestershire sauce. Cook for 10-15 minutes, till all ingredients are heated. Serve.

22 – Nicaraguan Beef Brisket Plantains - Baho

Baho translates to "steaming" or "to steam" in Spanish. The dish is made with yuca, plantains, beef brisket and various local vegetables. It is steamed to perfection in banana leaves.

Makes 8 Servings

Cooking + Prep Time: 5 hours + 24 hours marinating time

Ingredients:

- 1 x 4-pound thinly sliced brisket, beef
- 4 pounds of cassava
- 6 ripe plantains
- 3 green plantains
- Banana leaves
- 2 cups of orange juice, bitter
- 5 halved garlic cloves
- 5 onions, large
- 1 1/2 pounds of peeled, de-seeded, sliced tomatoes
- 1 sliced red, small bell pepper
- 1 sliced green, small bell pepper
- Salt, kosher
- Pepper, ground
- 1 bag of cabbage salad (coleslaw mix)

Instructions:

1. Halve the onions.

2. Season meat using kosher salt. Place in large bowl.

3. Add bitter orange juice, garlic and onions. Marinate mixture for 24 hours.

4. The next day, wash meat quickly, removing excess salt.

5. Cut marinated onions in thin slices.

6. Peel cassava and plantains. Halve them all.

7. Line large baking dish with the banana leaves. Allow them to overhang a bit. Do not leave any openings between leaves.

8. Form three layers:

9. Add cassava first.

10. Add ripe and green plantains. Place in standing position.

11. In middle area, place meat. Cover it with onions, tomatoes and bell peppers. Fold leaves over and close them.

12. Add 2 1/2 cups filtered water around ingredients. Boil on med. heat for about two hours.

13. Lower heat. Cook for two additional hours. Add more water as needed.

14. Each single serving of Baho includes one piece each of green and ripe plantains, one portion of meat and one piece of cassava. Top with prepared coleslaw mixture and serve.

23 – Traditional Nicaraguan Stew - Indio Viejo

This dish dates back to Nicaragua in the pre-Columbian era. The onion was added more recently, but most of the ingredients are native to Central America.

Makes 5 Servings

Cooking + Prep Time: 1 1/4 hour

Ingredients:

- 4 tbsp. of butter, unsalted
- 1 chopped onion, large
- 4 minced cloves of garlic
- 3 chopped bell peppers, any color is fine
- 5 chopped tomatoes
- 1 bunch mint
- 1 pound of beef or chicken
- 2 cups of flour, corn, mixed in 1 cup filtered water
- 2 cups beef or chicken broth
- Paprika or achiote, as desired
- 1 squeezed lemon, fresh
- Kosher salt, ground pepper and chili flakes, as desired

Instructions:

1. Heat the butter in large sized pot on med-high. Add garlic and onion. Stir them well and allow to cook for five minutes. Add the chicken. Allow to cook for five minutes per side.

2. Add mint, bell peppers and tomatoes. Stir again. Cook for eight to 10 more minutes.

3. In separate bowl, add broth and water to the corn flour you diluted. Stir, making sure you don't have any lumps.

4. Remove chicken from pot and shred it. Pour back in pot.

5. Add corn mixture to pot. Add paprika and/or achiote, as desired. Cook for eight to 10 minutes till chicken has fully cooked.

6. Add lemon juice. Season as desired. Stir till mixture is thoroughly combined. Add your favorite toppings. Serve soup alone, or with tortillas or rice.

24 – Shredded Beef - Ropa Vieja

You can make this dish quite easily in your Instant Pot. It's inspired by cooks and homemakers in Nicaragua, and the shredded beef is tender and delicious.

Makes 2 Servings

Cooking + Prep Time: 20 minutes

Ingredients:

- 3 tbsp. of oil, olive
- 1 cut onion – 1/2 of onion sliced lengthways and 1/2 sliced in large wedges
- 1 pepper, red – 1/2 of pepper sliced lengthways and 1/2 sliced in large wedges
- 1/2 sliced lengthways green pepper
- 2 sliced lengthways tomatoes, medium
- 2 lbs. cut in three pieces flank steak
- 1/2 bitter orange, juice only
- 2 1/2 cups of stock, beef
- Salt, kosher and pepper, ground, as desired
- 1/4 cup ketchup, low sodium
- 1 tbsp. mustard, yellow
- 1/2 tbsp. achiote – dilute in a bit of broth
- 2 tsp. Worcestershire sauce, reduced sodium
- 2 garlic cloves

Instructions:

1. Season flank steak as desired. Place all three steak pieces in inner liner of Instant Pot.

2. Add large wedges of onion, large wedges of green pepper, whole garlic and beef stock.

3. Place lid on your Instant Pot. Turn Steam Release valve to the Sealing setting. Cook on Manual setting for 12-15 minutes. After Instant Pot has finished, do Quick Release of steam.

4. Remove lid carefully. Remove steak from broth. Reserve broth in separate container.

5. Allow beef to rest for several minutes. Shred it.

6. Return inner liner to Instant Pot. Click on Sauté setting. Add oil. Wait till panel in front reads Hot.

7. Once Instant Pot has beeped, add lengthways sliced onions, tomatoes and peppers. Cook for three to five minutes, till barely tender.

8. Add shredded beef back to inner liner. Mix vegetables and beef.

9. Add one or two cups of the reserved broth to beef. Add diluted achiote, mustard, ketchup, lemon juice and Worcestershire sauce. Season as desired. Sauté for three to five minutes more. If sauce seems dry, you can add a little more of the reserved stock.

10. Serve with side of plantains, mashed potatoes or rice.

25 – Nicaraguan Vigoron

Vigoron is made with boiled cassava root (yuca), topped with cabbage salad and pork rinds. It's a wonderful light dinner or appetizer.

Makes 4-6 Servings

Cooking + Prep Time: 50 minutes

Ingredients:

- 2 lbs. of fresh cassava (yuca root)
- 1 bag of coleslaw mix
- 1 lb. of pork rinds

Instructions:

1. Cut ends of yuca root with sharp knife. Cut yuca in four-inch pieces. Remove skin like you do when you cut skin off oranges, revealing segments.

2. Rinse peeled yuca. Place in large sized pot. Fill pot with filtered water that covers yuca fully. Bring to simmer on med-high. Cook till it is tender, or 1/2 hour. Be sure you don't overcook yuca.

3. After yuca has cooked fully, remove it from water. Place on cutting board. Slice in small cubes. Discard fibrous pieces of yuca.

4. Place cubes of yuca on individual bowls or plates. Top with pork rinds and coleslaw mixture. Serve promptly.

26 – Churrasco Chicken

This dish is another national favorite in Nicaragua. Chimichurri is quite the traditional condiment. The Latin American rub is what **Makes** it a meal to remember. It can also be made with beef or pork.

Makes 6-8 Servings

Cooking + Prep Time: 25 minutes

Ingredients:

- 6 garlic cloves
- 3 bay leaves
- 2 chopped jalapeno chilies, with their seeds
- 1 1/2 tbsp. of salt, kosher
- 1/2 cup of minced parsley, curly
- 1/2 cup of minced parsley, flat leaf
- 1/4 cup of minced oregano, fresh
- 1/4 cup of vinegar, white, distilled
- 1/3 cup of oil, olive
- 5-lbs. of chicken, wings, legs, breasts
- Salt, kosher
- Pepper, black, ground

Instructions:

1. To prepare chimichurri, combine jalapenos, bay leaves, garlic and kosher salt in mortar. Mash with pestle till it forms a smooth paste. Transfer it to medium bowl. Add oregano and all parsley. Whisk in oil and vinegar till combined well and set it aside.

2. Prepare grill for med-hot. Oil grate lightly.

3. Cut chicken pieces into pieces of roughly 2 1/2" thickness. Season with kosher salt and ground pepper generously on both sides.

4. Place the chicken on grate. Grill for three minutes per side if you want it med-rare. There should be no pink remaining.

5. Transfer chicken to serving plate and serve it with chimichurri sauce on the side.

Desserts

Desserts are part of the culture in Nicaragua. Here are some of the most delicious…

27 – Crème Caramel – Latin Caramel Custard

Crème caramel is also known as Flan, and it's a commonly served dessert in Latin America. Originally it was brought to the region by settlers from Spain and France – it's simple but elegant.

Makes 6 Servings

Cooking + Prep Time: 1 3/4 hour

Ingredients:

- 1 cup of sugar, granulated
- 1/4 cup of water, filtered
- 4 beaten eggs, large
- 1 x 14-oz. can of milk, sweetened condensed
- 2 cups of water or low-fat milk
- 1/2 tsp. of vanilla, pure
- 1/2 cup of sugar, granulated

Instructions:

1. Preheat the oven to 350F. Place 1 cup of sugar plus water in heavy sauce pan. Stir and dissolve sugar well. Place on med. heat. Boil sugar and do not stir, till it begins turning honey brown in color.

2. Remove caramelized sugar from the heat. Pour into 9" cake pan. If you don't need all the sugar, that's fine.

3. Beat eggs, vanilla, 1/2 cup of granulated sugar, milk and condensed milk in large sized bowl. Pour into cake pan.

4. Place pan in oven. Cook till you can insert a knife in middle of custard and have it come back clean. Be sure you don't cook it too long.

5. Remove pan from oven. Allow flan to chill thoroughly. Run knife around edges. Invert over serving dish. Serve.

28 – Fancy Pastry - Rosquillas

Rosquillas are doughnut shaped pastries that are rather like Italian biscotti. They are often served with coffee, and many Nicaraguans allow them to float in their coffee for 30 seconds before eating.

Makes 100 small pastries

Cooking + Prep Time: 1 hour 10 minutes

Ingredients:

- 3 pounds of queso seco Nicaraguan cheese – You can substitute Queso Cotija de Montana cheese from Mexico if you need to.
- 3 pounds masa
- 2 eggs, large
- 4 tbsp. butter, unsalted
- 4 tbsp. beef lard
- 2 tbsp. pork lard
- Powdered sugar, for dusting

Instructions:

1. Preheat oven to 350F.

2. Grate cheese finely. Mix with masa.

3. Add both lards, eggs and butter. Mix till ingredients are combined well.

4. Knead dough several times before you roll it out. Roll into 1/2" thickness.

5. Use roll to create doughnut-shaped, small rosquillas. Place on baking sheets.

6. Bake pastries in oven till they get just a bit of color.

7. Remove rosquillas from oven. Allow to cool.

8. Heat oven to 200F. Return rosquillas to oven. Bake till crispy. Dust with powdered sugar and serve.

29 – Three Milk Cake – Pastel de Tres Leches

This is the cake of three milks, and many people believe it was first made in Nicaragua. It's very popular in Central America. The three types of milk give it a dense, rich quality.

Makes 8-10 Servings

Cooking + Prep Time: 2 hours 5 minutes + 2 to 8 hours refrigeration time

Ingredients:

- 1 1/2 cups of flour, all-purpose
- 1 tsp. of baking powder
- 1/2 cup of butter, unsalted, at room temperature
- 3/4 cup of sugar, granulated
- 5 eggs, large
- 1/2 tsp. of vanilla, pure
- 1 cup of milk, whole
- 1 cup of milk, sweetened condensed
- 2/3 cup of evaporated milk
- Whipped cream frosting, prepared

Instructions:

1. Preheat the oven to 350F. Grease, then flour 8x11" baking pan.

2. Sift baking powder and flour in large sized bowl. Cream butter and granulated sugar together on med. speed of mixer till fluffy and light.

3. Reduce speed of mixer to med-low. Add eggs, one after another. Incorporate each egg before you add another. Add vanilla. Beat till foamy.

4. Remove bowl from the mixer. Fold in sifted flour till incorporated well.

5. Pour batter into pan. Bake for 1/2 hour, till done. Remove pan from the oven. Set it aside and allow it to cool.

6. Pierce all parts of cake with fork. Mix all milks together. Pour over entire cake.

7. Refrigerate for two to eight hours, till cake has absorbed all liquid and is chilled well.

8. Frost cake. Serve. Since it's made with milk, this cake is perishable, so store any leftovers in your fridge.

30 – Yuca Doughnuts

These are yummy doughnuts made with yuca/cassava. They are fried, then served with a sweet, cinnamon and lemon syrupy sauce.

Makes 12 Servings

Cooking + Prep Time: 35 minutes

Ingredients:

For syrup

- 1 1/2 cups water, filtered
- 2 1/2 cups sugar, granulated
- 2 cinnamon sticks
- 1 lemon, juice only

For dough

- 2 cups cassava/yuca, grated
- 1 cup cheese, grated
- 1 egg, large
- 1/2 tsp. baking powder
- To fry
- 2 cups of cooking oil

Instructions:

1. Place ingredients for syrup, except lemon juice, in large sized pot.

2. Let mixture cook at 220F till syrup will coat a spoon.

3. Add the lemon juice, then mix well and set pot aside.

4. Mix ingredients for dough in large sized bowl.

5. Allow mixture to rest for 10-12 minutes.

6. Scoop dough in your hands. Form small balls by hand.

7. Heat the oil to 350F. Fry balls in hot oil.

8. Once balls are a golden-brown color, drain on plates lined with paper towels to absorb extra oil.

9. Drench doughnuts in warm syrup. Serve.

Conclusion

This Nicaragua cookbook has shown you...

How to use different ingredients to affect unique Nicaraguan tastes in dishes both well-known and rare.

How can you include Nicaraguan recipes in your home repertoire?

You can...

- Make delicious Nicaraguan breakfasts, which I don't imagine everyone has heard about. They are just as tasty as breakfast in other areas of the world.
- Learn to cook with plantains, which are widely used in Nicaragua. They are used in many types of dishes in Central America.
- Enjoy making delectable seafood ceviche and other fish dishes of Nicaragua, including fresh water fish. It's is a mainstay in the region and there are SO many ways to make it great.
- Make dishes using cassava, or yuca, which is often used in Nicaraguan cooking.

- Make various types of desserts like flan and three-milk cake, which will tempt your family's sweet tooth.

Have fun experimenting! Enjoy the results!

Author's Afterthoughts

Thanks ever so much to each of my cherished readers for investing the time to read this book!

I know you could have picked from many other books, but you chose this one. So, a big thanks for reading all the way to the end. If you enjoyed this book or received value from it, I'd like to ask you for a favor. Please take a few minutes to **post an honest and heartfelt review on** *Amazon.com.* Your support does make a difference and helps to benefit other people.

Thanks!

Julia Chiles

About the Author

Julia Chiles

(1951-present)

Julia received her culinary degree from Le Counte' School of Culinary Delights in Paris, France. She enjoyed cooking more than any of her former positions. She lived in Montgomery, Alabama most of her life. She married Roger

Chiles and moved with him to Paris as he pursued his career in journalism. During the time she was there, she joined several cooking groups to learn the French cuisine, which inspired her to attend school and become a great chef.

Julia has achieved many awards in the field of food preparation. She has taught at several different culinary schools. She is in high demand on the talk show circulation, sharing her knowledge and recipes. Julia's favorite pastime is learning new ways to cook old dishes.

Julia is now writing cookbooks to add to her long list of achievements. The present one consists of favorite recipes as well as a few culinary delights from other cultures. She expands everyone's expectations on how to achieve wonderful dishes and not spend a lot of money. Julia firmly believes a wonderful dish can be prepare out of common household staples.

If anyone is interested in collecting Julia's cookbooks, check out your local bookstores and online. They are a big seller whatever venue you choose to purchase from.

Made in the USA
Middletown, DE
09 October 2020